conquer
your stress

CARY L COOPER AND
STEPHEN PALMER

Ca **Cooper** is currently BUPA Professor of Organizational Psychology
ar u ealth in the Manchester School of Management, and Pro-Vice-
C ia: ellor (External Activities) of the University of Manchester Institute
c S nce and Technology (UMIST). He is the author of over 80 books (on
ccu ational stress, women at work and industrial and organisational
syc logy), has written over 300 scholarly articles for academic journals,
and a frequent contributor to national newspapers, TV and radio. His
Fell vships include the British Psychological Society, the Royal Society of
Art the Royal Society of Medicine, the Royal Society of Health, and the
(A erican) Academy of Management. He is President of the British
Ac lemy of Management and is a Companion of the (British) Institute of
Mc agement. He has been an advisor to the World Health Organization
an the ILO.

hen **Palmer** is Founder Director of the Centre for Stress Management,
lon, and Honorary Professor of Psychology at City University in the
re for Health and Counselling Psychology. He is a Strategic Director of
rofessional Development Foundation. He has written or edited 20 books
ress management and counselling. He edits or co-edits a number of
ssional journals and is Associate Editor of the *British Journal of Medical*
i. *ology*. Currently he is President of the Institute of Health Promotion
ar _ducation and Honorary Vice-President of the International Stress
Ma igement Association (UK). His fellowships include the British Association
for Counselling and the Royal Society of Arts. He is a consultant and trainer
to a number of leading international companies including BP Amoco.

Management Shapers is a comprehensive series covering all the crucial management skill areas. Each book includes the key issues, helpful starting points and practical advice in a concise and lively style. Together, they form an accessible library reflecting current best practice – ideal for study or quick reference.

The Chartered Institute of Personnel and Development is the leading publisher of books and reports for personnel and training professionals, students, and all those concerned with the effective management and development of people at work. For full details of all our titles, please contact the Publishing Department:

tel. 020-8263 3387
fax 020-8263 3850
e-mail publish@cipd.co.uk

The catalogue of all CIPD titles can be viewed on the CIPD website:
www.cipd.co.uk/publications

conquer
your**stress**

CARY L COOPER AND
STEPHEN PALMER

Chartered Institute of Personnel and Development

First published in 2000
Reprinted 2001

Design by Curve
Typesetting by Paperweight
Printed in Great Britain by
The Guernsey Press, Channel Islands

British Library Cataloguing in Publication Data
A catalogue record for this book is available from the
British Library

ISBN
0-85292-853-X

Chartered Institute of Personnel and Development, CIPD House,
Camp Road, London SW19 4UX
Tel.: 020 8971 9000   Fax: 020 8263 3333
E-mail: cipd@cipd.co.uk   Website: www.cipd.co.uk
Incorporated by Royal Charter. Registered charity no. 1079797

contents

dedication

To all my postgraduate students, past and present, who worked with me and made a real contribution to our understanding and knowledge of workplace stress. (CC)

To Maggie, who has supported me for almost two decades. (SP)

Other titles in the series:

introduction

- Feeling stressed?

- Having difficulty managing pressures?

- Procrastinating when you have important projects to complete?

- Never seem to have enough time for work or play?

- Suffering more from coughs and colds recently?

- Generally act in a passive or aggressive manner?

- Unable to concentrate?

- Becoming forgetful?

- Low self-esteem or self-worth?

- Easily angered?

- Generally irritable?

If you recognise any of the above, then this book is for you. Unlike most books on stress management, this one will explain exactly why you act in stress-inducing ways and make your life – and possibly others' – a misery at times. Do you ever wonder why, as soon as you are given an important project to work on, you find yourself tidying up your home

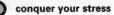

or office or start comfort-eating? Why do you make mountains out of molehills, and how can you stop this unhelpful approach to mismanaging your levels of stress? Do you recognise those 'musts' and 'shoulds' you regularly use against yourself and others to add intolerable pressure and stress to life? How often are you in a situation where you say out loud, 'I can't stand it any more'? Yet there you are, living proof that you *can* stand it!

This book, written by two stress experts, gives an in-depth insight into the causes of stress and how to conquer them. What may surprise you is how much we are directly responsible for our own levels of stress. The good news is that this puts the reader in an advantageous position of being able to reduce levels of stress if and when necessary.

The book is divided into five chapters. Chapter 1 looks at what stress is and provides a working model of stress that underpins the approach of the book. Chapter 2 takes a psychological approach to conquering stress and provides many strategies for dealing with our stress-inducing perceptions, attitudes and beliefs. This will really help to take the trauma out of a crisis. Chapter 3 concentrates on modifying our unhelpful behaviour by improving our interpersonal and time-management skills, and teaching us not to overlook the importance of support networks. Chapter 4 focuses on such physical health issues as exercise, nutrition and relaxation strategies. Finally, Chapter 5 helps to develop an action plan so we can become stress managers. It also helps us to assess whether we are a stress carrier and whether we wish to become a life manager, too. The Appendix contains a list of useful books and organisations that work with stress and stress management.

We should like to add an important caveat to this book. If you are suffering from undiagnosed physical or psychological symptoms, don't suffer in silence: consult your medical practitioner. If you attempt a stress management strategy from this book and find it unhelpful or anxiety-provoking, then don't use it. It you are suffering from very high levels of stress, we should recommend that you seek help from an appropriately trained professional, such as a psychologist or therapist (see the list of useful organisations, pages 85–7).

This book could seriously help you to reduce your levels of stress. Give it a go and see what happens!

what is stress?   1

So what is stress? It is one of those terms that means many things to many people. For the purposes of this book, it may be a good idea if we have a common understanding. In this chapter we shall provide you with a definition of stress, a working model of stress, and a section covering the major symptoms and causes of stress. You will be able to give yourself a quick stress audit, too!

Simple definition

There are many definitions of stress. The one we have found useful is:

Stress occurs when pressure exceeds your perceived ability to cope.

So it is not just external pressure, such as reaching deadlines, that leads to stress, but whether you believe that you can cope with a situation that you perceive as important or threatening. Obviously, the more experienced or skilled you are at a particular activity, such as giving presentations or completing projects on time, the less likely you are to become stressed. However, if you do not perceive that the problem is important or threatening then, even if you do not successfully deal with it, you are unlikely to become stressed.

Costs of stress

The costs of stress are immense. Surprisingly, stress has overtaken the common cold as a major reason for absence from work, and the Confederation of British Industry (CBI) has estimated that absenteeism costs British industry more than £10 billion a year. This is typical of many studies in the Western world. The effects of stress upon the individual are not encouraging, and studies have found it may be responsible for a variety of ailments, including:

- hypertension/high blood pressure

- heart attack/strokes

- ulcers

- diabetes

- angina

- cancer

- rheumatoid arthritis

- psychological disorders, including breakdowns.

Model of stress

Let's consider a modern model of stress. The diagram on page 8 provides a useful framework that is broken down into a number of stages. We shall focus initially on the first three stages. Stage 1 is usually a life event or external pressure that has come to the person's attention. Some of the more serious life events include being laid off work, bereavement and illness. During Stage 2, if the person perceives this event or pressure as stressful, then this triggers the old evolutionary 'fight or flight' stress response. However, if the person believes that they have the ability to deal with the demand, then they perceive the situation as a challenge and so not as anything stressful. In fact, they may quite enjoy facing it and feel excited.

At Stage 3, the three key responses to stress are activated: the psychological, behavioural and physiological. The physiological response includes the release of stress hormones such as adrenaline and noradrenaline which prepare the heart, lungs and major muscle groups for action – for either fight or flight. Fats and sugars are also released into the blood to provide energy.

Have a look now at the model of stress diagram and also Activity 1 before reading on.

Model of stress

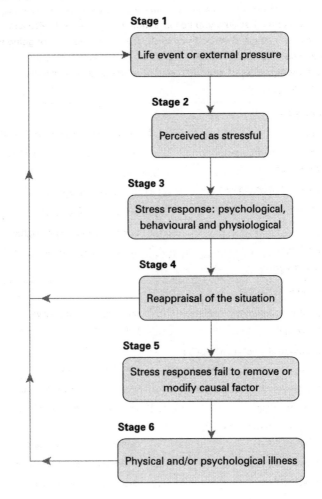

Adapted from Palmer and Strickland (1996)

Activity 1   Self-assessment of your stress response

Think back to the last time you became moderately stressed. (You can choose a very stressful event if you wish, as long as you are not going to overly upset yourself.) Tick the symptoms below that you recognise. If you are feeling stressed now, then tick those that you are currently experiencing.

Psychological

- ❏ angry
- ❏ anxious, apprehensive, frightened
- ❏ ashamed, embarrassed
- ❏ depressed or feeling low
- ❏ guilty
- ❏ jealous
- ❏ mood swings
- ❏ reduced self-esteem, self-worth
- ❏ feeling out of control, helpless
- ❏ suicidal ideas
- ❏ paranoid thinking
- ❏ unable to concentrate
- ❏ intrusive images or thoughts
- ❏ increased daydreaming

Behavioural

- ❏ passive or aggressive behaviour
- ❏ irritability
- ❏ increased alcohol consumption
- ❏ increased caffeine consumption (eg tea, coffee)
- ❏ comfort-eating
- ❏ disturbed sleep patterns (eg waking up early)
- ❏ withdrawing or sulking
- ❏ clenched fists
- ❏ banging surface (eg table) with fists
- ❏ compulsive or impulsive behaviour
- ❏ 'checking' rituals
- ❏ poor time management
- ❏ reduced work performance
- ❏ increased absenteeism from work
- ❏ eating/talking/walking fast
- ❏ increased accident-proneness
- ❏ change in interest of sex
- ❏ nervous tics

Physiological/physical

❑ frequent colds or other infections	❑ indigestion
❑ palpitations or thumping heartbeat	❑ diarrhoea
	❑ constipation
❑ breathlessness	❑ skin complaints or allergies
❑ tightness or pain in the chest	❑ asthma
❑ feeling faint or fainting	❑ excessive sweating or clammy hands
❑ migraines	
❑ vague aches	❑ change to the menstrual pattern
❑ tension headaches	❑ rapid weight change
❑ backaches	❑ thrush or cystitis

This exercise will help you to become aware of your responses to stress.

Which symptoms occurred first? In future, use these symptoms as an early-warning sign that you are possibly suffering from stress and may benefit from some action on your part. If you are experiencing more than five of the above symptoms on a regular basis, you may wish to receive further advice from your medical practitioner. Some of the more serious symptoms, such as chest pains or suicidal ideas, need more urgent attention.

The list is just a guide. Some of the symptoms you have ticked may reflect an organic problem that needs medical assistance.

Now you have increased understanding of your response to stress we can return to the model of stress. In Stage 4, the person reappraises the original situation and decides whether or not they have successfully resolved it. If it is resolved or being managed, then the stress response is usually switched off. However, if the person believes that they are not coping with the stress scenario, then the psychological, behavioural and physiological responses may persist.

Stage 5 focuses on whether the person has modified, removed or otherwise dealt with the external cause(s) of stress over a period of time. If the life event or external stress factor has not been successfully dealt with, physical or psychological illness(es) may ensue (Stage 6). If this occurs it can exacerbate an already difficult situation and feed back into the top of the diagram. For example, if a person has not successfully resolved problems at work and has underperformed for six months, it is very likely that their employer will provide negative feedback or may even resort to a disciplinary procedure. This can have in turn a devastating effect on a person's self-esteem, and, as they become clinically depressed, their work deteriorates even more, leading finally to dismissal.

Pressure and stress

Research has shown that there is a physiological difference between *pressure* and *stress*. A person experiencing stress has higher levels of the various stress hormones in their bloodstream than a person who feels merely challenged.

Activity 2   Pressure and stress

Think back to the last time you were stressed. How did you feel? What symptoms did you suffer? Did you enjoy the experience?

Now think back to the last time you felt challenged but not overwhelmed. How did you feel? What symptoms did you suffer? Did you enjoy the experience?

When people are feeling appropriately challenged they often feel excited about accomplishing a task, whereas when they are stressed they usually experience a range of negative thoughts, feelings and physical sensations (see Activity 1, pages 9–10). The right amount of pressure for a person is good, whereas stress has many negative manifestations that are seldom good for anybody.

Occupational and organisational stress

This section may be of interest to readers in work. Due to increased workplace litigation, employers are taking occupational and organisational stress more seriously. Do you recognise any of the following symptoms at work:

- ❏ low morale
- ❏ industrial relations difficulties
- ❏ high absenteeism
- ❏ increase in long-term illness
- ❏ increased or high turnover of staff
- ❏ increased litigation
- ❏ reduced efficiency
- ❏ poor performance in tasks
- ❏ poor quality-control
- ❏ deadlines not being reached

❏   increased bullying

❏   increase in accidents

❏   long-hours culture?

Research has indicated that there are six main areas that can cause occupational stress. Activity 3 will help you assess the causes of stress at your employment.

Activity 3   Assessment of the causes of occupational and organisational stress

Tick the following items that you recognise in your current place of work. (You may wish to consider a previous employment too.)

Relationships

❏   deteriorating or difficult relationships with boss, manager, colleagues, subordinates or customers

❏   bullying

❏   passive or aggressive colleagues or managers

❏   conflicts

❏   harassment

❏   abrasive personalities

❏   office politics

❏   lack of social support

Organisational structure and climate

❏   lack of communication

❏   inadequate communication

❏   hierarchy

❏   too little supervision

❏   too much supervision

❏   lack of control

❏   lack of autonomy

❏   racism

❏   sexism

❏   homophobia

❏   inadequate co-ordination

❏   inconsistent style of management

❏   reduced staffing levels

❏   inflexible working procedures

Factors intrinsic to the job

- ❏ person–job mismatch
- ❏ poor environment
- ❏ poor ventilation
- ❏ open-plan offices
- ❏ inadequate lighting
- ❏ workplace temperature too hot or too cold
- ❏ excessive noise
- ❏ poorly designed equipment and machines
- ❏ new technology
- ❏ excessive number of e-mails
- ❏ static electricity
- ❏ pollution
- ❏ smoke and other toxic substances
- ❏ hazardous work
- ❏ long hours
- ❏ shift work, unsocial hours
- ❏ VDU screen glare
- ❏ isolation
- ❏ lack of personal security
- ❏ poor childcare facilities

Role in the organisation

- ❏ excessive responsibility
- ❏ lack of responsibility
- ❏ role overload
- ❏ role underload
- ❏ role ambiguity
- ❏ role conflict

Career development

- ❏ overpromotion
- ❏ underpromotion
- ❏ demotion
- ❏ low status
- ❏ lack of job security
- ❏ threat of lay-offs
- ❏ enforced early retirement
- ❏ retraining necessary
- ❏ thwarted ambition
- ❏ short-term contracts
- ❏ job relocation

Home–work interface

- ❏ stress at work affecting home life
- ❏ stress at home affecting performance at work
- ❏ dual-career family
- ❏ conflicting careers of partners

Total the number of items you ticked. In our experience, employees who tick more than about 10 of these items are likely to be suffering from stress to varying degrees, unless they are really not concerned about their jobs. For some employees, just the threat of losing their jobs is sufficient to trigger high levels of stress.

Activity 3 may have raised a number of issues for you. Spend a few minutes thinking about which items relating to yourself you could make an effort to manage or resolve, ignoring the items that are beyond your control. Consider how you may go about implementing changes at work regarding these problem areas.

If you believe that there are high levels of stress at work that are not being dealt with, you may wish to encourage your employers to take the matter more seriously. We list below a number of interventions that you could consider making:

● Check whether colleagues agree with your point of view. Discuss the issue of stress with them. Perhaps show them the list of individual symptoms (pages 9–10) and the list of organisational stressors (pages 13–14).

■ Investigate whether your organisation already has a stress policy.

▲ If you and your colleagues do feel that stress exists, consider discussing this issue with your supervisor, manager or director, or with a representative from occupational health, training, human resources/personnel or the appropriate trade union.

● Set up a working party of colleagues interested in assessing the levels of stress and in developing (if needed) a stress management programme.

● Consider in what ways your organisational culture contributes to stress.

● Undertake a stress audit to discover the levels of stress. Use a professional consultancy or suitably qualified colleagues in-house. Consider how to manage the important issue of confidentiality with regard to stress questionnaires. If staff do not believe that their individual answers will remain confidential, they are less likely to complete them.

■ Stress management or managing pressure workshops or courses can help employees. In addition, a focus on dealing with the causes of stress at work, such as a long-hours culture or aggressive managers, may be beneficial.

Review

In this chapter we have provided an overview of what stress is, the symptoms experienced by individuals and organisations, and some ideas about dealing with occupational stress.

At the end of each chapter we recommend that you make a note of the problems you wish to deal with and any useful strategies that will help you to conquer or at least manage stress. This will help you to develop your own conquering stress Action Plan.

Notes

changing your thinking 2
to conquer stress

In the previous chapter we answered the question, 'What is stress?' It may have surprised you to learn that your perceptions about events or your thinking style and attitudes can also contribute to your levels of stress. In this chapter we shall show you how to examine your stress-inducing thinking errors and apply problem-solving thinking skills to most situations. We shall provide you with a toolkit of psychological techniques and strategies.

The influence of our perceptions over how stressed we become is not a modern concept. As the first-century philosopher Epictetus noted: 'People are disturbed not by things, but by the views which they take of them.' Centuries later, Shakespeare proffered a similar sentiment: 'there is nothing either good or bad, but thinking makes it so' (*Hamlet* II.ii).

So what was their solution to dealing with stressful situations? Marcus Aurelius, a second-century Roman Emperor and philosopher, suggested that our internal 'assessor' could be challenged:

Refuse its assessment, and all is well... Everything is what your opinion makes it; and that opinion lies with yourself. Renounce it

when you will, and at once you have rounded the foreland and all is
calm: a tranquil sea, a tideless haven.

During the past hundred years Sigmund Freud's
psychoanalytical theory has greatly influenced Western
society. The popularised interpretation of Freud has led many
of us to believe that others, especially our parents, are to
blame for how we feel and the way we act. Yet, if we take
seriously the suggestion by the ancient philosophers that all
we need to do is change or modify our thinking, then we are
put firmly back in the driving seat, which enables us to deal
with the inevitable stress and pressures of daily life.
According to Aurelius, by mentally reappraising a situation
we can feel calmer and less stressed. This approach has
received a lot of attention over the past 40 years from
psychologists who have undertaken many research studies
to confirm that this method works for a range of stress-related
problems.

As simple as ABC!

So what exactly is the sequence of events that leads to stress?
Four decades ago, Dr Albert Ellis, an internationally
renowned psychologist, put forward the following model:

The ABC model of stress

A   Activating event
or situation

B   Beliefs about
the event

C   Consequences:
    emotional, eg anxiety
    behavioural, eg aggression
    physiological, eg palpitations

Notice that this is similar to the first three stages of our model of stress (see page 8). This ABC model allows any situation that you become stressed about to be analysed. Activity 4 will hopefully illustrate this procedure.

Activity 4   Your thoughts when stressed

Think back to the last time you became stressed. Perhaps you were stuck in a traffic queue or had just been asked by a colleague to give a presentation to the board of directors. Perhaps your computer had just crashed.

Bring the incident back to mind as clearly as you can. What ideas or thoughts were going through your mind at the time?

If you felt angry, did you label either yourself or the other person as a 'total idiot'?

If you were anxious or stressed, did you think that the situation was 'awful' or 'terrible'?

If you really did not like the situation, did you perhaps demand that things 'should be better' or that 'My boss must not treat me this way'?

Perhaps you avoided the situation. If this was the case, did you tell yourself that 'I really can't stand it any more'?

If you had these thoughts, did they help you to become less stressed or did they exacerbate the situation? In fact, did you become more able to solve problems or less able? We suspect the latter.

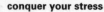

What insights, if any, did you glean from Activity 4? The majority of people we have tried this exercise with are normally quite surprised at how their thoughts tended to make the situation worse. Regardless of the Activating event or stressful situation, psychologists have found that we hold a number of Beliefs that are self-defeating and task-interfering in nature.

We have developed a simple self-assessment questionnaire to help you discover which of your beliefs can create or exacerbate stressful situations (adapted Palmer, 1999).

In our experience, if a person holds on strongly to one of the beliefs listed in the SIBI (see pages 23–4) then, when an event occurs that does not live up to expectations, stress may result. Therefore, the more beliefs you hold strongly or even moderately, the more stress you are likely to encounter. Do note that 'shoulds', 'musts', 'have tos', 'got tos' and similar demanding ideas you may hold are interchangeable. So if instead of a 'should' you use a 'must', this will still rate on the questionnaire. If you scored more than 10 strongly, it is very likely that *you* make many situations into potential stress scenarios! If more than 15, this section of the book is really for you. Even if you hold any of the above beliefs only moderately, under extremes of pressure you are likely to become quite stressed.

Stress-inducing beliefs indicator (SIBI)

Do you recognise any of the following? The questions include both work and general beliefs. Circle the strength of your belief, where S represents strongly, M represents moderately and W represents weakly. Include in Question 25 any additional beliefs you hold that cause you further stress.

1	S	M	W	Events should go smoothly
2	S	M	W	Work must be exciting and stimulating
3	S	M	W	If I lost my job, life would be 'awful'
4	S	M	W	If I lost my job, I could not bear it
5	S	M	W	My job is one of the most important things to me
6	S	M	W	I must perform well at all important tasks
7	S	M	W	My work should be recognised by others
8	S	M	W	I am indispensable at work
9	S	M	W	I must enjoy myself whatever I'm doing
10	S	M	W	I must not get bored
11	S	M	W	I should not encounter problems
12	S	M	W	I should have the solitude I deserve
13	S	M	W	I must escape from responsibilities and demands
14	S	M	W	I should be treated fairly
15	S	M	W	I should be treated as special
16	S	M	W	I should be in control of all significant situations
17	S	M	W	Others should respect me
18	S	M	W	I should get on well with my friends and family
19	S	M	W	My children should do well in life
20	S	M	W	If things went badly, it would be 'awful'
21	S	M	W	If things went badly, I could not stand it
22	S	M	W	Things never work out well for me
23	S	M	W	If things go wrong, those responsible are 'stupid', 'useless', 'idiots' or 'failures'

| 24 | S | M | W | If I fail at a task, that proves I'm a failure or useless |
| 25 | S | M | W | Additional beliefs: _____ |

_____

Thinking errors

So what is the answer? Psychologists have identified 14 thinking errors that frequently contribute to stress and hinder successful problem-solving. Our approach to dealing with them is in two stages:

1 Identify the thinking errors you most commonly use.

2 Use thinking skills to help modify the errors.

Activity 5 will help you undertake Stage 1 of our approach.

Activity 5   Thinking errors

Think back to the last time you were moderately stressed. Tick or highlight the following thinking errors that you recognise.

All-or-nothing thinking We view things in absolute, extreme terms without any shades of grey.

Examples
If a job is worth doing, it is worth doing well.
My partner always makes the same mistakes.

Labelling We 'globally rate' ourselves, others or the universe, as opposed to rating skills deficits or specific behaviours.

Examples

Because I've failed my professional exams, this proves I am a failure and
totally stupid.

She's late again. This is more evidence that she's incompetent.

Focusing on the negative Instead of keeping life or events in perspective,
we focus only on the negative aspects.

Examples

Things are always going wrong in my job.
Our child is always causing us problems.

Discounting the positive We choose to reframe anything positive as
unimportant.

Examples

When my manager gives me positive feedback she is only saying it to be
nice. She doesn't really mean it.

My partner only tells me that he loves me because he feels sorry for me.
He doesn't really care.

Mind-reading We infer from people's behaviour that they are either
thinking or reacting negatively towards us.

Examples

I'm sure my colleagues think that I can't undertake this project
successfully.

My neighbour has ignored me again He must have seen me in the
garden. What have I done to upset him?

Fortune-telling We predict the worst-case scenario, often by using
insufficient evidence.

Examples

I've got off to a bad start today. That means the rest of the day will be a
write-off too!

What's the point in going on holiday? The weather is bound to be awful.

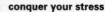

Magnification or 'awfulising' We have a tendency to blow the significance of events out of proportion and make mountains out of molehills.

Examples

If we don't reach that deadline, the outcome will be awful.
If she leaves me, it will be the end of my world.

Minimisation We condemn ourselves for our shortcomings and make excuses for our successes or strengths.

Examples

I was lucky. Getting the contract was nothing, really.
The exams I passed were easy ones.

Emotional reasoning We evaluate situations by how we feel.

Examples

I feel so angry, it proves that he treated me badly.
I feel so anxious about flying, it must be dangerous to fly.

Blame Instead of taking any personal responsibility, we blame others for problems that may have occurred.

Examples

It's all the managing director's fault: she shouldn't have given me so
    much work.
Where are my socks? Who has moved them?

'Personalisation' We may blame ourselves unfairly for something for which we are not totally responsible.

Examples

My staff did not reach the target. It's all my fault.
My partner has left me and I am totally to blame.

'Demanding-ness' This occurs when we hold unrealistic expectations or rigid and absolutist beliefs usually expressed as 'shoulds', 'musts', 'got tos', 'have tos' and 'oughts'.

Chartered Institute of Personnel and Development

Customer Satisfaction Survey

*We would be grateful if you could spend a few minutes answering these questions and return the postcard to CIPD. <u>Please use a black pen to answer</u>. **If you would like to receive a free CIPD pen, please include your name and address.*** IPD MEMBER Y/N

....

1. Title of book ....

2. Date of purchase: month ....   year ....

3. How did you acquire this book?
☐ Bookshop   ☐ Mail order   ☐ Exhibition   ☐ Gift   ☐ Bought from Author

4. If ordered by mail, how long did it take to arrive:
☐ 1 week   ☐ 2 weeks   ☐ more than 2 weeks

5. Name of shop ....   Town... Country ....

6. Please grade the following according to their influence on your purchasing decision with 1 as least influential: (please tick)

	1	2	3	4	5
Title					
Publisher					
Author					
Price					
Subject					
Cover					

7. On a scale of 1 to 5 (with 1 as poor & 5 as excellent) please give your impressions of the book in terms of: (please tick)

	1	2	3	4	5
Cover design					
Paper/print quality					
Good value for money					
General level of service					

8. Did you find the book:
Covers the subject in sufficient depth   ☐ Yes   ☐ No
Useful for your work   ☐ Yes   ☐ No

9. Are you using this book to help:
☐ In your work ☐ Personal study   ☐ Both   ☐ Other (please state)

Please complete if you are using this as part of a course

10. Name of academic institution..

11. Name of course you are following? ....

12. Did you find this book relevant to the syllabus? ☐ Yes ☐ No   ☐ Don't know

Thank you!

To receive regular information about CIPD books and resources call 020 8263 3387.

Any data or information provided to the CIPD for the purposes of membership and other Institute activities will be processed by means of a computer database or otherwise. You may, from time to time, receive business information relevant to your work from the Institute and its other activities. If you do not wish to receive such information please write to the CIPD, giving your full name, address and postcode. The Institute does not make its membership lists available to any outside organisation.

1795/05/00

21

BUSINESS REPLY SERVICE
Licence No WD 1019

Publishing Department

Chartered Institute of Personnel and Development

CIPD House

Camp Road

Wimbledon

London

SW19 4BR

Examples

I must perform well regardless of the lack of resources.

My partner and I should never row with each other.

'Phoney-ism' We fear others may find out that we are not the person we portray.

Examples

Even though so far I have given good lectures, one day I'll make a
mistake and they will discover how incompetent I really am.

When my children grow up they will realise what a hopeless parent I
was.

'I-can't-stand-it-itis' We lower our tolerance for dealing with adversity or frustrating situations by telling ourselves that 'I can't stand it' or 'I can't bear it.'

Examples

I can't stand travelling on the Underground in the rush hour.

I can't bear small rooms or noisy children.

Activity 5 should have helped you recognise a number of thinking errors that you make. On reflection, do you think that there are any that you regularly apply to many situations? In the next section we shall provide a range of thinking skills and strategies to help you challenge and modify these errors.

The ABCDE of thinking errors and skills

Thinking skills can be used to help you challenge inaccurate perceptions about events or the 14 common thinking errors previously covered. But how do they fit into the ABC model of stress we described earlier?

In fact, Dr Albert Ellis added an additional stage to his ABC model, which we highlight below:

The ABCDE model of stress

A   Activating event
or situation

B   Beliefs about
the event

C   Consequences:
emotional, eg anxiety and stress
behavioural, eg aggression
physiological, eg palpitations

D   Disputation of the beliefs at 'B'

E   Effective new approach to deal
with the activating event at 'A'

Once we note down our stress-inducing beliefs and thinking errors at 'B', we can start to dispute or challenge them at 'D' and subsequently develop new stress-coping statements along with an effective new approach to help us deal with the problem.

Activity 6

So far, so good! The hard work starts now. To help you practise the thinking skills, we suggest that you think about either a previous stress scenario or a current problem you are stressed about. Note down your stress-inducing and task-interfering beliefs. Complete Table A by noting down the thinking errors you recognise (see the previous section). (You may wish to include thinking errors that you regularly make too.)

Table A Thinking errors audit

Thinking errors	*Your example*
All-or-nothing	
Labelling	
Focusing on the negative	
Discounting the positive	
Mind-reading	
Fortune-telling	
Magnification or 'awfulising'	
Minimisation	
Emotional reasoning	
Blame	
'Personalisation'	
'Demanding-ness'	
'Phoney-ism'	
'I-can't-stand-it-itis'	

Now you have completed Activity 6, you should be in a position to start tackling your thinking errors or incorrect perceptions. Below we list a few methods to help you modify your stress-inducing thinking. Use one or more of these thinking skills to help challenge your thinking errors.

Relative thinking

If you are perceiving events in extreme terms, such as 'excellent *v* poor', try to introduce shades of grey – find some middle ground to help you keep the situation in perspective.

Examples

Instead of thinking 'She never reaches her targets', be more realistic: 'Although this year she has failed to reach two targets on time, she has successfully achieved eight others.'

Instead of thinking 'If a job's worth doing, it's worth doing very well', introduce a less extreme attitude: 'Within the time and resources I have available, I'll do a reasonable job.'

Befriend yourself

If a member of your family or a colleague makes an error, how do you react? Most people are supportive; therefore we can say they possess befriending skills. However, how often do you use these skills on yourself? When you make a mistake can you accept yourself or do you become ultra-critical and metaphorically beat yourself up?

Example

Instead of thinking 'That was a hopeless presentation. That proves I'm totally useless', step back from the situation and describe it more accurately: 'Some aspects of my presentation were not particularly good. However, this does not prove that I'm totally useless. In fact, I now know what areas I can focus on to improve my next presentation.'

De-labelling

When you describe either yourself or somebody else as 'a total failure', 'useless', 'stupid', 'an idiot', 'a fool' or a similar 'global rating', examine your idea more closely. Is it really an accurate description? To be a 'total failure' what would a person have to do all the time, day and night? Think carefully before you answer. Yes, you may have the correct answer! The person would have to fail at *absolutely everything* to be a 'total failure'. Obviously this is extremely difficult, if not impossible, to achieve.

Examples

Instead of thinking 'I have failed my exam, therefore I am a complete failure', focus on the behavioural deficit and avoid going as far as a global rating of yourself: 'All it proves is that I've failed my exam – no more, no less. Tough; too bad; I can survive this hassle.' Another example is to think 'Although I've acted stupidly, this does not mean I'm stupid.'

When you are angry about another person's action, again rate the *behaviour* and not the person: 'Although my manager has interpersonal skills deficits, it does not make him a total idiot.'

Broaden the picture

Instead of focusing on the negative and discounting the positive, start concentrating on more realistic and positive aspects of a situation. When things go wrong, individuals too often blame either themselves (personalisation) or an innocent bystander. So, whatever situation you find yourself in, attempt to broaden the picture when blame enters the equation. First, write down all the different factors or people involved. Second, draw a circle on a large sheet of paper. Third, using the circle, draw a pie diagram, with each section approximately equating to the fault or responsibility of the different factors or people involved. Finally, whatever is left of the pie diagram is probably your responsibility.

Seek evidence

Avoid mind-reading or making assumptions. Look for the evidence for and against your stress-inducing ideas. This may involve asking your family, friends or colleagues for feedback about something you may have done, such as giving a presentation, completing a task, or some personal issue. If you believe that your manager or partner really does not like what you are doing or have done, ask them to share their thoughts with you. Avoid beating about the bush. Ask a direct question. You can also challenge your thinking behaviourally.

Example

If you believe that 'I can't stand queuing', when you next find yourself in a situation when you have to queue, join the longest one. Instead of making yourself angry and wound up, remind yourself that 'Although I don't like queuing, I'm living proof that I can stand it!'

Thinking more flexibly

Dogmatic, inflexible, absolutist and demanding beliefs trigger high levels of stress. Introduce flexible beliefs such as preferences, desires and wants into your repertoire.

Examples

Instead of thinking 'I must perform well', 'I should achieve my deadlines regardless of the lack of resources' or 'My children have to do well at school', attempt to become more flexible in your thinking style. 'It's strongly preferable to perform well, but realistically I don't have to'; 'Although it's highly desirable to achieve my deadlines, with the current lack of resources I can only do my best'; or 'Of course I want my children to do well, but demanding that they have to can only make the situation worse. Let's give myself and them a break.'

Demagnify or 'deawfulise'

Whatever the situation, if you blow it out of proportion, you are very likely to increase your stress levels. Of course, events may be difficult to deal with, or even be plain bad, but are they really 'the end of the world', 'horrendous', 'awful', 'horrible'? Seldom are events we face on a day-to-day basis that bad. To examine stress scenarios dispassionately, we recommend that you distance yourself from your immediate stress-inducing thinking to help you see the wood from the trees.

Example

'It's really terrible that I failed my driving test.' Now, if you examine the situation just described, all that has happened is that a person has failed their driving test. This may be a hassle but, keeping it in perspective, is it really a terrible event? No! However, in their own mind the person has elevated a hassle into a horror, which leads to unnecessary stress. A realistic view would be 'I've failed my driving test. Tough; too bad. It's just a great inconvenience – no more, no less.'

Keeping emotions in their place

As we described earlier, when people make the emotional reasoning thinking error, they evaluate a situation on the strength of their feelings and not on the situation itself. In the previous section on emotional reasoning (page 26) we described two classic examples where emotions can cloud a person's judgement. We suggest that it is important to remind yourself that just because you are feeling a strong emotion such as anxiety, it does not necessarily mean that you are in a threatening situation or have been treated badly when you are feeling angry.

Examples

'Just because I'm feeling anxious it does not mean that flying is dangerous.'

'Perhaps I feel very angry because I misinterpreted my partner's actions. I'll ask him what it was all about.'

To summarise, thinking skills are used to promote *realistic* rather than positive thinking; things may be bad, but seldom are they really awful, unless we allow our thinking to make them so!

Helpful challenging questions

Now that we have introduced you to some of the key thinking errors and thinking skills, you may wonder what we do as psychologists when we are either coaching or counselling individuals who are feeling stressed. In addition to the skills we have discussed in the previous section, we also help such people to become their own self-coach. Once they have identified the ABCs of the problem according to Dr Albert Ellis' model, we provide them with a list of helpful questions they can use to challenge their own stress-inducing ideas. You can give this self-help approach a go now, in Activity 7.

Activity 7   Helpful challenging questions

This activity involves a number of steps:

Step 1 Think of a situation you are or have been stressed about (for example, missing a deadline). Note this down. This is your *A*ctivating event.

Step 2 Next, note down both how you felt and your behaviour – for example 'anxious', 'procrastinating'. These are your *C*onsequences.

Step 3 Now imagine the situation at *A* and get into the feelings you described at *C*. When you are feeling stressed, note down your stress-inducing thoughts. These are your *B*eliefs. Some of these may be self-defeating, because they hinder you and do not help you attain your goals.

Step 4 Let us now move on to *D*isputation, as described on page 28. This is when you dispute or challenge the thoughts or beliefs you noted down in Step 3 here, your *B*. Watch out for your thinking errors. To help you challenge your beliefs, we have provided in Table B the list of 'helpful challenging questions' we use with our stressed clients.

Table B Helpful challenging questions

- Is it logical?
- Would a scientist agree with my logic?
- Where is the evidence for my belief?
- Where is the belief written (apart from inside my own head!)?
- Is my belief realistic?
- Would my friends and colleagues agree with my idea?
- Does everybody share my attitude? If not, why not?
- Am I expecting myself or others to be perfect, as opposed to fallible, human beings?
- What makes the situation so awful, terrible or horrible?
- Am I making a mountain out of a molehill?

- ◎ Will it seem this bad in one, three, six or twelve months' time?
- ▣ Will it be important in two years' time?
- △ Is it really as bad a problem as a serious accident or a close bereavement?
- ◎ Am I exaggerating the importance of this problem?
- ◎ Am I fortune-telling again, with little evidence that the worst-case scenario will actually happen?
- ◎ If I 'can't stand it' or 'can't bear it', what will really happen?
- ▣ If I can't stand it, will I really fall apart!?
- △ Am I concentrating on my (or others') weaknesses and neglecting my (or others') strengths?
- ◎ Am I agonising about how things should be instead of dealing with them as they are?
- ◎ Where is this thought or attitude getting me?
- ◎ Is my belief helping me to attain my goal(s)?
- ▣ Is my belief goal-focused and problem-solving?
- △ If a friend made a similar mistake, would I be so critical?
- ◎ Am I thinking in all-or-nothing terms? Is there any middle ground?
- ◎ Am I labelling myself, somebody or something else? Is this logical, and a fair thing to do?
- ◎ Just because a problem has occurred, does it mean that I am (it is, they are) stupid, a failure, useless or hopeless?
- ▣ Am I placing demands (eg 'shoulds'/'musts' etc) on myself or others? If I am, is this proving helpful and constructive?
- △ Am I taking things too personally?
- ◎ Am I blaming others unfairly just to make myself (temporarily) feel better?

Select the questions that may help you to challenge your beliefs at *B* (in the ABC model of stress). It is important to ask yourself the question and then ponder on the possible answer for a while.

It is also worth noting that the questions could easily be boiled down to three main types:

1 Is the belief logical?
2 Is the belief realistic (empirically correct)?
3 Is the belief helpful (eg assisting you to achieve your goals)?

Once you have asked yourself the appropriate questions, modify the belief you held at *B* to one that is more logical, realistic and helpful. For example, try shifting your attitude from 'Missing the deadline is really awful' to 'Missing the deadline is a pain, but hardly awful. Frankly, I'm making a mountain out of a molehill' (a realistic and helpful stress-reducing belief). Note down this new belief.

Step 5 You have almost finished. Now note down your *E*ffective new approach to dealing with the situation. For example, make up for lost time by finishing the task now and don't waste any time fretting!

'Pros and cons' analysis

Another good method to help deal with the psychological slings and arrows that we hurl at ourselves when we are under pressure or stress is a 'pros and cons' analysis of our stress-inducing thinking. Writing up a 'pros and cons' list is a fairly straightforward procedure often used in the work environment to help managers decide what particular approach to take when attempting to solve a range of difficulties. We have modified it to focus on the validity and usefulness of the ideas or beliefs people hold when stressed.

Table C is an example of Jayne, a perfectionist, who wishes to start revising for her forthcoming professional exams. As is often the case with rigid perfectionists, she is procrastinating and not getting down to her studying. This situation is, furthermore, repeated at work when she has important deadlines to meet. Again, many perfectionists claim that they work best at the eleventh hour or under pressure – perhaps you do too! But we would argue that such people are not then at their best and, what's more, are very likely to make errors late at night! We can think of cases when rigid perfectionists have been so tired and flustered at midnight or minutes before a meeting that they forget to spell-check important reports or documents. Their perfectionistic approach ends up looking unprofessional! Let's look closely at Jayne's 'pros and cons' analysis, laid out in Table C.

Table C Jayne's 'pros and cons' analysis of her belief

Problem	Procrastinating, not studying
Belief	I must not fail my exams. If I did, I would be a failure, and that would be awful.
Goal	To start studying.

Pros	*Cons*
⊚ I shall do my best.	⊚ I am spending all my time worrying about failing my exams.
▨ I produced a really good plan for how I'm going to start on my revision.	▨ I've spent hours and hours planning my revision but I still have not started it properly yet!
△ My belief helps to motivate me.	△ It also helps to make me feel so anxious that I can't concentrate on my studies. I spend my time worrying about becoming a failure

and how awful that would be. In addition, I've spent many years of my life avoiding doing things that I might fail in.

○ My family will be so proud of me if I get a good pass.

○ If I stay anxious and stressed, I won't do well and they won't be proud of me.

○ My study is now spotless and the files on my PC are all in order.

○ The only way I can calm down is to tidy things up. But this is just wasting my precious time, which I can't afford to lose. I've even cleaned the kitchen floor twice today!

Perhaps you recognise in yourself all or at least some of Jayne's belief, 'I must not fail my exam. If I did, I would be a failure and that would be awful.'

Activity 8

To undertake this exercise we recommend that you place your most stress-inducing belief at the top of a sheet of paper and write your goal underneath. Then divide the remaining paper into the two sections, 'Pros' and 'Cons', and complete it in the same manner as Jayne. Once you have included all the 'pros and cons' you may wish to ask a friend or colleague to help you brainstorm additional ones. Once you have finished making the list, decide whether it is worth modifying your idea to a belief that is more flexible, self-helping and task-oriented. In Jayne's case she developed a new belief:

> *Although it's strongly preferable not to fail my exam, if I do then it doesn't prove I'm a failure, because I have many other worthwhile attributes. It may be a hassle, but it certainly isn't awful or the end of the world. I might as well just start revising now.*

This is a simple yet useful exercise that can be used with colleagues, partners and indeed children that needs only time, paper and a pen!

Overcoming the self-esteem trap

In Western society we have found that one of the main causes of stress for people of all ages is having a strong belief in the concept of self-esteem. This may sound somewhat remarkable, yet we see it daily in our work. In this section we focus on self-esteem and the healthier alternative known as *self-acceptance*.

Activity 9

Spend the next five minutes noting down on paper how you, your friends, colleagues and family build up their self-esteem. You may think that you are okay as a person for a number of reasons. State these reasons.

Activity 9 was probably an easy exercise to undertake. We have found that the main 'external' factors that people in Western society use to enhance their self-esteem are these (Palmer, 1997):

- achievement, eg passing exams etc
- having a good relationship with significant others
- having a rewarding and satisfactory job or career
- owning property
- possessing excellent physical characteristics
- being competent in personally significant areas
- being a good parent/grandparent/colleague/friend
- being a good lover, partner etc
- being loved by a significant other
- being approved of by significant others
- practising a religious faith.

Essentially, people tend to 'dis-esteem' themselves when they lose something personally significant, such as a job, a partner, good health or property, and conversely esteem themselves more highly when they have or acquire something personally significant, such as a good job, an attractive partner, a good physique, high IQ etc. So when a person says, 'I'm okay because…', that person is probably into the self-esteem trap. In concrete terms, some of the common examples of this trap are:

I'm okay because:

   – I'm attractive

- *I've got a good job*

- *I never lose my temper*

- *I'm a good parent*

- *I'm good in bed*

- *I've passed my exams*

- *I'm well qualified*

- *I have many friends*

- *I have a good sense of humour.*

However, all living human beings get older and possibly less attractive (look in the mirror and notice the thinning hair or wrinkles!); some may lose their jobs or have to retire; others may have negative personal attributes, be at times deficient in their parenting skills, lose their property, fail exams or lose friends through arguments or death. This is just a small selection of relevant personal aspects. We are sure that you can think of many more. Thus, the philosophy of esteeming one's self can set us up for potential problems in the future when adversity in almost any form strikes. It is no surprise that recent research has shown how teachers often blame poor media coverage and lack of governmental support as major contributory factors leading to reduced self-esteem and self-worth. So what is the alternative?

From the trap to self-acceptance

With self-esteem you feel good about yourself when life is

going well but bad when life is not going well. To avoid these ups and downs of self-esteem we suggest that learning self-acceptance can reduce much stress and literally provide people with a new sense of personal freedom. The concept of self-acceptance acknowledges that one of the key aspects that makes us human is that we are fallible and definitely not perfect. Therefore we could turn the earlier statement on its head by telling ourselves:

I'm okay just because I exist.

Although it may sound rather extreme, spend a few moments thinking about this idea. Would it take the stress out of many of those competitive situations that you have encountered or when you have lost something significant in your life?

Another helpful self-accepting belief might be this:

I can accept myself, warts and all, with a strong preference to improve myself, even though realistically I don't have to.

We have found that it is important, especially for people with perfectionist beliefs, still to keep their strong desire to perform well. Preferences, wants and desires are very healthy as long as the person does not demand that they 'must' achieve their desires. This helps the concept of self-acceptance to remain realistic, unlike self-esteem.

Another helpful self-accepting belief may be:

I am too complex to be rated.

This is a pretty remarkable idea that takes the stress out of many situations. Consider the implications when we translate this into a concrete example:

Instead of 'Because I have failed my exam I am a failure' (a global rating of self that leads to self-defeating stress, anxiety and depression), the alternative becomes 'Because I have failed my exam, all it proves is that I have exam skills deficits' (the rating of skills, leading to healthy and realistic disappointment but still retaining motivation).

Accepting others but not their behaviour

Think of the times when you have become angry about another person's behaviour, such as that of your partner, child, parent, colleague, manager or maybe even another driver. Did you globally rate and label them as 'useless', 'waste of space', 'stupid', 'idiot', or 'xxxxxxx!'? Or perhaps you kept relatively calm and accepted their fallibility by just rating such aspects as these:

On this occasion my child acted stupidly but this does not mean she is stupid.

My father has interpersonal skills deficits.

The driver is exhibiting driving skills deficits.

So, instead of stating that the other person 'should not' act in a particular way and, if they do, giving them a 'label' of some kind, you accept the empirical reality of their fallibility, which helps reduce your levels of stress, and possibly anger too. Incidentally, we are not suggesting that you accept their *behaviour* – just their fallibility. We shall show you how to deal with unwelcome behaviour in Chapter 3.

Activity 10

The next time you hear yourself globally rate either yourself or another person, use the situation as an opportunity to quickly start rating the *aspect* of yourself or the other person that you dislike, and not the individual in a global manner. Note whether this helps you to reduce your stress levels, thereby enabling you to deal with the situation in a more appropriate way.

Imagery exercises

We have observed that people are far less likely to deal successfully with a stressful or challenging situation if they have not prepared for it. This is common sense. Just imagine giving a presentation with inadequate preparation or not revising for an important exam! What would have been the outcome if you had not had lessons before your driving test? We suspect that you would have been very likely to fail.

Another observation worth making is that, prior to stressful events, people tend to have negative images or pictures in their mind's eye about how they are going to cope – or, to be more accurate, not going to cope – with the situation. These images of doom and gloom seldom reduce stress levels, so the person concerned gradually becomes more and more stressed prior to the event. This can even affect sleep, because the person finds it difficult to switch off at bedtime, and even if they do get off to sleep they often wake up early.

Fortunately, there are a number of imagery exercises that psychologists have developed to help most people deal with these problems. In the next section we shall provide three powerful methods to put you ahead of the stress game.

Coping imagery

This is probably one of the most effective stress-management techniques to help people deal with difficult situations or potential stress scenarios, and can even assist in extreme cases such as phobias. By imagining yourself coping with the feared situation you directly challenge the negative or catastrophic imagery that may be winding you up prior to the event. Notice that we have used the word 'coping' and not 'mastering'. This is crucial, because most people have little confidence in themselves actually performing perfectly and so have no belief in mastery imagery. Coping imagery enables you to accept that you may not be able to give that perfect presentation, be the life and soul of the party, make no errors at that important job interview, or make few mistakes when meeting your new partner's family or friends. What it does instead is use a step-by-step approach to help you deal with adversity. To grasp the basic technique, attempt Activity 11 on page 48.

Activity 11 Coping imagery

Step 1 Think of a future situation that you are stressed about.

Step 2 Note down the aspects of the situation that you are most stressed about.

Step 3 Develop ways to deal with these difficulties.

Step 4 Now carefully visualise yourself in the feared situation. Slowly picture yourself coping with each anticipated difficulty as it arises. Repeat this procedure three or four times.

Step 5 Practise Step 4 daily, especially when you become stressed about the forthcoming event.

The sticking point for some people is Step 3 – they are unable to develop ways to deal with the situation. In these cases we recommend that it may be helpful to discuss the problem with an experienced colleague, friend or family member. Remember, the idea is to deal with your worst fears and not to pretend that they simply may not happen.

For example, if you are most stressed about being asked difficult questions after giving a presentation, then focus on how you would deal with this situation should it occur. Perhaps you might decide the best strategy would be to inform the audience that you are unsure of the answer to the particular question but will get back to the person after the presentation. This strategy would then become the key aspect of the visualisation to practise in Step 4. To return to the classic example that triggers stress for many people, the driving test: the visualisation at Step 4 would include seeing yourself preparing for the day, having a driving lesson beforehand, meeting the test examiner, undertaking difficult manoeuvres and so on.

This method helps to prevent negative images creating high levels of stress, thereby becoming self-fulfilling prophecies. Many successful managers and caring parents have found that they can teach their staff and children coping imagery to deal with a range of problems. The latter find it particularly useful to calm nerves associated with examinations.

Self-motivation imagery

Motivation imagery is used to help people inspire themselves to action in whatever area of life they need a quick jump-start. It was developed by two psychologists, Palmer and Neenan, who found that many of their clients avoided life changes because they feared they would not be able to cope with the stress created.

Motivation imagery consists, first, of visualising the rest of your life not doing what you want to do and, second, of visualising actually doing what you want to do. Activity 12 provides the framework for using self-motivation imagery.

Activity 12 Self-motivation imagery

Spend a few minutes thinking about possible areas of your life that you could improve by taking action which you have avoided. Examples may include changing jobs or going for promotion; returning to study; finishing a significant relationship; writing a book; or challenging your manager, partner, parents or in-laws about some important issue. If you are unemployed, have you become disillusioned after receiving many 'rejections'?

Assuming you are not too depressed about the area of life you would like to change, undertake the exercise below. Once you start, it is important to work through all three steps.

Step 1 Visualise the rest of your life *not* having undertaken the change that you would like to. To assist in this exercise, imagine the effect upon yourself, and perhaps on significant others too, for the rest of your life until the day you die if you do absolutely nothing. Think of your regrets, too. Imagine the effect year by year.

Step 2 Now visualise yourself undertaking what you want to do and then see the short- and long-term positive benefits of the change to you and possibly others.

Step 3 Now consider how you are going to put Step 2 into action.

It is important that Step 1 (known as 'inaction' imagery) is visualised before Step 2 (known as 'action' imagery), otherwise it is possible you may demotivate yourself, which is not the intention of the exercise! Motivation imagery has helped to change people's lives and pull them out of a boring, stressful rut into a new and exciting domain.

Time projection imagery

So often people lose their perspective of a stressful situation, such as becoming unemployed, failing an exam, relationship break-ups or performing poorly. Becoming very stressed does not usually help them to deal with the situation in a constructive manner, and they often lose sight of their goals. Time projection imagery helps to keep the event in perspective, and so is a useful 'deawfulising' tool. Activity 13 explains how.

Activity 13 Time projection imagery

Step 1 Think of a problem or situation that you are stressed about.

Step 2 Picture yourself three months in the future. Will the current problem be as stressful as it is now?

Step 3 Picture yourself six months in the future. Will the current problem be as stressful or as important as it is now? Can you see yourself getting on with your life?

Step 4 Picture yourself 12 months in the future. Will the current problem be as stressful or as important as it is now? Can you see yourself getting on with your life?

Step 5 Picture yourself two years in the future. Will the current problem be as stressful or as important as it is now? Will you laugh at your problem when you look back at it? Can you see yourself having fun again?

Step 6 Picture yourself five years in the future. Will the memory and significance of the problem fade into the past? If you still find it difficult to imagine a positive future, picture having a new job or career, different friends, or whatever is appropriate.

The instructions for the imagery exercises we have covered in this chapter can easily be recorded onto an audio cassette tape which can be played when you are undertaking the activities. In Chapter 4, which focuses on health, we include another imagery method that helps physical and mental relaxation. If you are in desperate need of relaxation, go directly to page 75 and attempt Activity 20; then go to Chapter 3 once the exercise has been completed.

Review

Note down any problems that you wish to deal with and any useful strategies that will help you to conquer or manage stress.

changing your behaviour to conquer stress

3

Changing your behaviour to conquer stress sounds easy enough, but it usually involves hard work. What interests psychologists about human behaviour is why people do or do not do certain things. People may have the ability to be good time-managers, be assertive, and choose the right friends and colleagues for support. Yet they often decide *not* to apply these skills when they need them!

In this chapter we shall focus on three main behavioural areas: social support, assertion and time management. We shall also look at why we do not always use the skills we possess in stressful situations.

Social support

Research has highlighted the importance of social support networks that act as a buffer against stress. Assuming you have chosen the right person to speak to, work colleagues, family or friends can provide appropriate guidance and support when necessary.

Work problems often require somebody who is task-focused, whereas home-life difficulties often need a sympathetic ear, although it is not always this straightforward. Some people are deterred from talking to others about their problems, because they view it as a sign of weakness. They may even withdraw from supportive relationships, paradoxically, at a time when they most need them. We would view discussing our problems with appropriate others as a strength, because we are then more likely to keep our problems in perspective and resolve them.

Activity 14, which focuses on your support networks, may reveal your strengths and weaknesses in this area.

Activity 14 Support networks

When problems arise, which colleagues, friends or family members can you rely on for support? Make a list of these people for the different situations below:

- ⊙ a work problem
- ▣ a social or family problem
- ▲ when you are stressed or anxious
- ⊙ a crisis
- ⊙ a debt problem
- ⊙ difficulties with study.

Did you encounter difficulties writing this list? Did you find that you rely on only a few people for most of the problems? If you answered yes to either or both of these questions, you may wish to focus on this area of your life. You may never have needed to ask for guidance or help, but appropriate support can take the trauma out of a future crisis and support networks are worth developing.

Assertiveness training

It is very difficult to be a good time-manager without assertiveness skills – hence our focus on this topic before we examine the well-known method for conquering stress, time management.

Assertive behaviour involves being able to ask for what you want, stand up for yourself, complain appropriately, defend yourself and give constructive feedback to others when necessary. Hopefully, its use avoids such negative consequences as exploitation, resentment, misunderstanding and passiveness.

Activity 15 Behaviour

There are three types of behaviour that people tend to exhibit: aggressive, non-assertive (passive), and assertive. Tick the ones that you recognise in yourself.

Aggressive

Behaviour	*Phrases/words used*
◎ Finger-pointing	◎ You'd better...
▣ Leaning forward	▣ It's your fault
▵ Sharp, sarcastic or firm voice	▵ You're joking
◎ Fist(s)-thumping	◎ You ought/must/should...
◎ Loud voice/shouting	◎ Don't be stupid
◎ Violation of others' rights	
▣ Dominating demeanour	

Non-assertive/passive

Behaviour

- ⊙ Shrugging
- ▣ Hunched shoulders
- △ Whining, quiet or giggly voice
- ⊙ Hand-wringing
- ⊙ Shifting of body weight
- ⊙ Stepping backward
- ▣ Downcast eyes

Phrases/words used

- ⊙ Maybe
- ▣ Perhaps
- △ Just
- ⊙ Only
- ⊙ I wonder if you could...
- ⊙ I'm hopeless/useless
- ▣ I can't
- △ Never mind
- ⊙ It's not important
- ⊙ I mean...
- ⊙ Well, uh...

Assertive

Behaviour

- ⊙ Relaxed demeanour
- ▣ Lack of hostility
- △ Smiling when pleased
- ⊙ No fidgeting/slouching
- ⊙ Collaborative approach
- ⊙ Good eye-contact

Phrases/words used

- ⊙ Co-operative: let's, we could...
- ▣ Open questions: What do you think/want? How do you feel?
- △ 'I' statements: I think, I want, I fear, I feel

In Activity 15 the type of behaviour you tend to exhibit to others is indicated by the section in which you have the most ticks. We recommend that the aggressive and the non-assertive or passive behaviours are reduced and the assertive behaviours increased in any social interaction, thereby creating a win–win philosophy, as opposed to the more common win–lose. Being aggressive tends to wind up others as well as the person concerned, leading to conflict and resentment. Passive behaviour is tantamount to letting others walk over you, which tends to lead to reduced self-esteem and depression. It is worth noting that some people exhibit a passive–aggressive combination by having aggressive body behaviour but using passive language instead. They tend to be manipulative, sarcastic and cynical, although they may avoid direct conflict.

Assertiveness rights

The literature on assertion usually recognises a number of assertiveness rights. Do you agree that you have the right to:

- say no
- consider your needs important
- make mistakes
- take responsibility for your behaviour
- express your feelings in an appropriate manner without violating anybody else's rights
- set your own priorities
- be understood
- be you
- be assertive without feeling guilty
- respect yourself?

If you disagree with any of these assertiveness rights, try discussing the particular 'right' with a trusted friend or colleague and obtain their views.

Assertiveness skills

There are a number of assertiveness skills you may wish to attempt at the next appropriate opportunity. We outline the key skills under the headings below.

Workable compromise

You offer the other person(s) a compromise, assuming that your self-worth or self-respect is not being challenged. For example:

Your manager: We are getting desperately behind. Can you come in on Saturday morning and finish the paperwork?

You: I've agreed to take my daughter horse-riding tomorrow morning, and I'm not prepared to let her down. However, I can start work earlier next Monday and do my best to get the work finished. Is that OK?

Negative enquiry

Instead of receiving just global, negative feedback, negative enquiry encourages the other person to provide specific information about your behaviour in a more constructive manner. For example:

Relative: You are a totally hopeless parent!

You: Can you share with me in what way I am hopeless?

Broken record

This involves stating your viewpoint in a relaxed manner while ignoring irrelevant logic or arguments, manipulative traps or baiting. For example:

Student: You are being really unfair. Why should my results suffer just because my project came in late?

Tutor: Unfortunately, the regulations state that a project has to be submitted on the due date; otherwise marks are taken off.

Student: You've never liked me from the start of the course. I bet you let others off.

Tutor: The regulations apply to everybody. Marks are taken off if a project is submitted late.

Fogging

By simply acknowledging your mistakes, this skill helps when others are using 'put-downs' or manipulative criticism. This helps you to maintain your self-respect. For example:

Manager: Late again! You're letting the office down.

You: Three months ago I was late when the train broke down and, unfortunately, it happened again today.

These examples show how assertiveness skills can be applied to a range of situations. Many people have the skills but choose not to use them for a variety of reasons, including fear of upsetting others because they are 'people pleasers'; having low self-worth and so usually putting others' wants first; or having a desire for others to like them. If you recognise one or more of these issues, you may wish to return to Chapter 2 and examine the thinking errors you are possibly making.

Assertiveness skills are not always recommended, because their use by some people can increase the likelihood of violence occurring or because an employer may use their being deployed as an excuse to dismiss the person. In these situations an alternative course of action may be necessary.

Time-management

If you can manage your time successfully, you are more likely to control or conquer the majority of your stress at home and at work. Now that we have considered thinking skills (in Chapter 2) and how to be assertive (in this chapter), time-management should become easier to use on a daily basis. However, we need first of all to consider why people procrastinate.

Activity 16 Do you procrastinate?

Think back to the last time you had an important project to complete, essay to write, exam to study for or presentation to give. Did you waste any time doing any of the things listed below? Tick the behaviours you performed:

- ❏ cleaning and tidying your desk
- ❏ dusting or tidying your room or VDU
- ❏ cleaning the kitchen floor
- ❏ washing the windows
- ❏ cutting the grass
- ❏ weeding the garden
- ❏ cleaning the car
- ❏ talking to distant relatives
- ❏ responding to unimportant e-mails
- ❏ playing computer games
- ❏ spending an inordinate amount of time making a priority list
- ❏ spending days preparing the work by obtaining yet more background information
- ❏ tidying the filing system (whether filing cabinets or your computer files)
- ❏ doing the unimportant jobs in the in-tray
- ❏ answering unnecessary telephone calls
- ❏ consuming more drinks, food or cigarettes than usual
- ❏ whinging to colleagues about the amount of work you have
- ❏ blaming your boss or others
- ❏ telling others that you work best at the eleventh hour (or even later!)

So why do many people under pressure procrastinate? Look at the graph on page 62. As soon as a person has to do something that they want to do well at, their stress levels often increase. However, when they start cleaning the floor, doing the unimportant things in the in-tray or whatever, their stress levels temporarily drop. Yet, some time later when they finish procrastinating and think about the job in hand, their stress levels rise even higher than before as they realise that they have wasted valuable time.

The stress curve

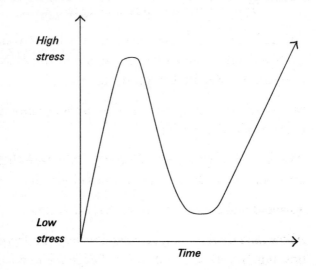

The key is to recognise initially that you *are* procrastinating – in other words, doing something that is *not* directly focused on helping you to achieve your goal. If you also recognise a thinking error such as labelling, eg 'If I fail my exam I'll be a failure', then challenge it (see Chapter 2).

Sometimes people procrastinate for another reason: there is a boring task they need to complete. In these cases the thinking error is generally 'I can't stand doing boring jobs.' Therefore the 'I can't-stand-it-itis' should be challenged (see Chapter 2).

Top tips for the time manager

- At the beginning of the week, make a list of your goals and targets, and prioritise. Revise the list daily, as necessary. Regularly refer to the list.

- Spend only an appropriate amount of time planning your workload or project.

- Avoid procrastinating. Challenge the thinking errors or beliefs that underpin this behaviour.

- To avoid making errors, do one task at a time.

- Allow time for the unexpected and be realistic about how much work you and your colleagues can do.

- Avoid automatically saying yes to others' requests. With time-consuming projects, ask yourself whether you really need to agree to the request being asked. Use assertiveness skills; say no when necessary.

- When possible, deal with incoming postal mail or e-mails as soon as you open them or, if under pressure, consider prioritising them and deal with the unimportant mail later.

- Group outgoing telephone calls together. List items to be discussed and be precise.

- Prepare for meetings and list items you wish to discuss.

Review

Note down any problems that you wish to deal with and any useful strategies that will help you to conquer or manage stress.

improving your physical health to help you conquer stress

4

There are a number of key strategies you can undertake to help deal with your physiological response to stress. In this chapter we shall focus on exercise, nutrition and physiological relaxation methods. The short self-assessment questionnaire in Activity 18 will indicate whether this chapter is for you or whether you may be better off proceeding to Chapter 5.

Activity 18 Healthy living self-assessment questionnaire

Against each question below circle the answer that applies to you, where 'S' represents seldom or never, 'O' represents occasionally and 'F' represents frequently.

Exercise scale

1	S	O	F	Do you undertake physical exercise, such as jogging or cycling?
2	S	O	F	Do you take part in sports activities that involve physical exertion?
3	S	O	F	Do you integrate exercise into your daily routine?
4	S	O	F	Do you feel exhausted after little physical exertion?

Nutrition scale

5	S	O	F	Do you drink more than five cups of coffee a day?
6	S	O	F	Do you drink more than eight cups of tea a day?

7	S	O	F	Do you eat three meals a day?
8	S	O	F	Do you eat between meals?
9	S	O	F	Do you eat fruit and vegetables?
10	S	O	F	Do you binge-drink alcohol?
11	S	O	F	Do you eat foods high in saturated fats?

Relaxation scale

12	S	O	F	Do you use such relaxation techniques as meditation?
13	S	O	F	Do you use imagery exercises to help you relax?
14	S	O	F	Do you feel physically tense?
15	S	O	F	Do you have migraines, backaches or headaches?

Miscellaneous

16	Yes	No	Are you under- or overweight?
17	Yes	No	Do you drink in excess of the recommended weekly guidelines for alcohol (14 units for women, 21 units for men)?
18	S	O	F	Do you smoke?

Desirable answers

1	F	7	F	13	O or F
2	O or F	8	S	14	S
3	F	9	F	15	S
4	S (If O or F, check with your GP.)	10	S (preferably never!)	16	No
				17	No
5	S	11	S	18	S (preferably never!)
6	S	12	O or F		

If you answered any question with an undesirable response you may wish to reconsider that area of your life. This chapter will focus on most of the relevant topics.

Exercise

There are many benefits from taking exercise. These include improving your physical and mental health, stress-busting, anger control, weight control, reducing depression and enhancing your self-esteem. For many people, exercise works by distracting them from their difficulties and problems, especially if it involves team games.

However, before you decide to take up some form of vigorous exercise such as jogging or playing squash please note the following: if you are over 35, pregnant, convalescing or overweight, or you have asthma, bronchitis, high blood pressure (hypertension), chest pains, diabetes or a family history of heart disease, it is imperative that initially you seek advice from your medical practitioner.

Exercise pointers

Avoid overdoing it! Grade your training programme into manageable chunks. Avoid setting yourself difficult goals. If you feel nauseous, dizzy or in pain, stop exercising immediately.

If your training programme is enjoyable, you are more likely to maintain it over a period of time. Perhaps exercise with family, colleagues or friends – but avoid being competitive!

Warm up with gentle bends and stretches before you start your training programme.

Allow for a cool-down period after exercise. Walk slowly for a few minutes.

Choose a range of exercises, some of which are not weather-dependent.

When using exercise equipment, try listening to your favourite music or radio programmes to avoid boredom.

It is not advisable to undertake arduous exercise within one or two hours of eating a heavy meal.

Choose sports facilities that are easily accessible from your home or work.

Integrate exercise into your everyday routine. At work use the stairs instead of the lift or escalator.

Don't give up your training programme just because you have missed it for a few days or weeks owing to work or home pressures. Use the thinking skills discussed in Chapter 2 to challenge your exercise-interfering beliefs.

Nutrition

Why should we be careful about our diet? Poor nutrition that is lacking in the essential vitamins and minerals but includes saturated fats can lead to a range of serious disorders such as heart disease. Although a busy lifestyle can interfere with our eating habits, a healthy, balanced diet should be a goal to achieve whenever possible. In this section we focus on food to eat and food to avoid!

Heart disease and fats

A diet rich in saturated fats increases the risk of heart disease because fatty deposits (known as blood cholesterol or low-density lipoproteins) adhere to the arterial walls, which can lead to narrowed and eventually blocked arteries. This raises blood pressure and may finally result in a heart attack. Not all fats are potentially dangerous; therefore we shall describe the main ones below.

Saturated fats

A number of products contain the sorts of saturated fat that can lead to heart disease, including cheese, milk, lard, hard margarine and butter. The fatty sections of pork, lamb and beef also contain high levels of saturated fats.

Mono-unsaturated fats

Although classed as fats, the mono-unsaturated fats do not increase blood cholesterol levels, or the sticky, low-density lipoproteins. The main source of these fats is olive oil and avocado pears. Some research has indicated that olive oil may be one of the key factors responsible for the low rate of heart disease found among Mediterranean people. Olive oil is now included in some margarines.

Polyunsaturated fats

Polyunsaturated fats are found in such oily fish as pilchards, mackerel and sardines. Their main benefit is that they help to prevent blood clots from forming and reduce blood cholesterol levels. Another type of polyunsaturate is found in vegetable oils, such as soya, sunflower, corn and safflower. Some margarines are labelled 'high in polyunsaturates', and are to be preferred to butter or lard.

Foods to cut down on

● Fried food.

■ Meat products, eg burgers, pâtés, pork scratchings, sausages and meat with fatty portions.

▲ Canned fruit in syrup.

● Full-fat cheeses such as Cheddar or Stilton.

● Biscuits, white bread and sweetened breakfast cereals.

● Whole milk, cream and yogurt (unless low-fat natural yogurt).

■ Products with a high sugar content, eg chocolate, sweetened fruit juices, instant custard and some cola drinks.

▲ Salt or products with a high salt content. Consult your medical practitioner, initially, if you have low blood pressure.

● Mayonnaise and salad dressings that are oily and low in polyunsaturates or olive oil.

Preferred foods

- Poached, steamed or grilled food.

- Fish, poultry or lean meat. Oily fish is particularly healthy.

- Fruit, eg apples, bananas, grapes, oranges, or fruit in natural juices.

- Low-fat cheese, cottage cheese or alternatives made with sunflower oil.

- High-fibre products that aid the digestion, including beans, bran, wholegrain bread, brown rice, cereals, pasta and oats.

- Semi-skimmed or skimmed milk.

- Mayonnaise alternatives or salad dressings low in fat or high in polyunsaturates.

Interesting research

Although we would not encourage you to drink large quantities of tea, recent research has found that drinking between two and five cups a day reduces the risk of strokes. Somewhat surprisingly, dark chocolate helps to lower cholesterol levels. One or two units of alcohol a day reduce the stickiness of blood, making it less likely to clot and cause a thrombosis. Because these are easy, health-related changes to instigate, you may wish to consider adding them to your review at the end of this chapter.

Weight control

Most diets do not work. Dieters temporarily reduce weight and then put it back on again. The key to controlling body weight is to understand a simple equation: body weight is increased when energy intake exceeds energy used. Therefore, if you are overweight, to achieve the desired weight for your height you will need to reduce your calorific input by eating less food and expending more energy by increasing your lifestyle activity and undertaking more exercise. Once achieved, the desired weight can be maintained by keeping a correct balance between calories consumed and energy expended. Basically, it is that simple!

Lifestyle changes that help this process include avoiding snacks between meals; cutting out from your diet foods high in fats and sugars; and incorporating exercise into your daily routine, such as walking or cycling to work or to the shops, and taking part in sports such as tennis or badminton. (Bear in mind, however, that building up muscles can lead to weight gain.)

Obesity should be taken seriously, because it can lead to heart disease, stroke, high blood pressure, gallstones, arthritis, diabetes and bronchitis. It really is worth bothering about.

Relaxation

There are a number of different relaxation techniques that help to reduce the physical effects of stress and tension. If you already use yoga, massage, mediation or imagery exercises successfully then you may not need to read this section.

We provide here a couple of methods that many tens of thousands of people have found useful. The methods work by helping the person to switch off mentally, thereby enhancing the parasympathetic nervous system, which aids relaxation, and the digestive and immune systems. Interestingly, research has shown that meditative techniques can lead to 50 per cent fewer visits to hospital either as an in- or out-patient. If at any time when you are using these techniques you do not like the sensation of relaxation, open your eyes and the feelings will quickly pass.

Benson relaxation technique

This Western form of meditation was developed by H. Benson, who found that it could reduce blood pressure and hypertension. A number of your choice is used as a mantra, which helps to block out unwanted thoughts. What follows here is a modified version that the authors have found helpful.

Activity 19 Benson relaxation technique

Step 1 If possible, find a noise-free place and reduce the level of lighting. Ensure that you will not be disturbed.

Step 2 Find a comfortable position and lie down or sit quietly.

Step 3 Close your eyes.

Step 4 Relax your muscles in groups. Start at your face and progress down to your toes.

Step 5	Focus on your breathing. Breathe naturally in through your nose and out through your mouth. Notice how your stomach may rise and fall as you breathe in and out. Avoid letting your shoulders rise as you breathe.
Step 6	In your mind, say a number such as 'one' every time you breathe out.
Step 7	Continue for five to 20 minutes.
Step 8	Finish in your own time.

A golden rule of relaxation is *not* to try hard. With regular practice it will come naturally but, like any new skill, it may take several attempts. If you are keen to learn more about relaxation techniques, meditation or yoga, try your local adult education college or obtain a good relaxation audiotape from a reputable dealer.

Relaxation imagery

Relaxation imagery is an excellent method to help achieve a relaxed state of body and mind. It involves picturing in your mind's eye one of your favourite relaxing places. The scene can be real or imaginary – sunbathing on a beach, walking through a park, taking a relaxing bath. Activity 20 describes the procedure.

Activity 20 Relaxation imagery

Step 1 Find a quiet place where you are unlikely to be disturbed. If possible, reduce the level of lighting.

Step 2 Find a comfortable position and lie down or sit quietly.

Step 3 Close your eyes and picture one of your favourite relaxing places.

Step 4 Focus on the colours in your relaxing place.

Step 5 Focus on one colour in particular.

Step 6 Focus on the sounds or silence in your relaxing place.

Step 7 Imagine touching something in your relaxing place.

Step 8 Focus on any aromas or smells in your relaxing place.

Step 9 In your own time, open your eyes.

Anyone who regularly practises this method will be able to achieve a relaxed state relatively quickly and with little effort.

Review

Note down any problems that you wish to deal with and any useful strategies that will help you to conquer or manage stress.

---

developing your own action plan

5

Having (we hope) read all the previous chapters and undertaken some of the Activity exercises, you will now be in a position to develop your own action plan and therefore be only a few steps away from becoming a 'life manager'. However, there are a few loose ends to tie up before we arrive at the action plan, and we shall now focus on them.

'Stress carriers'

When you are under pressure at home or at work, how do you react? Do you:

- rush around like a headless chicken
- become irritable
- bang tables or desks with your fist
- become aggressive
- stop making pleasantries with family and colleagues
- sulk or withdraw
- blame others
- shout at yourself or others

- become cynical or sarcastic
- deny reality
- 'awfulise' about the possible outcome
- start bullying others?

If you do any of the above, what is likely to be the effect on your friends, colleagues, partner or family? Do they become more helpful or less so? Do you motivate or demotivate others? Does your behaviour help you to achieve your goals, whatever they are, when you are under pressure?

In our experience, people exhibiting a number of the above behaviours tend to be a trigger of stress in others around them, which leads to greater stress or inefficiency (or both) within a team or family. In recent years people like this have been called 'stress carriers', owing to their negative effect upon others close at hand. In extreme cases they may not notice any effect on themselves and sadly be unaware of their impact upon others. Similar to typhoid Mary, who did not succumb to the effects of typhoid yet infected many of her customers, stress carriers often inflict stress upon anybody they come into contact with but themselves survive (in the short term) remarkably unscathed.

If you believe that you have a tendency to be a stress carrier, you may wish to consider which behaviours you should target for action.

Home–work interface

In our experience, people who are encountering occupational stress are unlikely just to leave it at work. It usually has an effect on their personal life, because they are unable to switch off their problems on arriving home. They do not necessarily kick the cat as they return from work, but they may be irritable and angry or just withdraw into themselves and prefer the television for company. Likewise, if partners are having relationship difficulties or sleepless nights because their baby keeps them awake, this can adversely affect their work life. Either way, the home–work interface often needs to be managed carefully to ensure that there is little or no overspill from one to the other. Strategies discussed in earlier chapters may need to be applied, such as thinking skills, imagery and relaxation exercises, and assertiveness skills.

Action plan

When you are going to go shopping you probably make a list of what you wish to purchase. If you are organising a wedding or managing a project, then you are again very likely to plan goals and targets.

Developing your own conquering stress action plan is no different.

Activity 21 Review

Look back through the previous chapters at the Activity exercises. Note down any areas that relate to your general thinking skills or skills deficits, behaviour or physical health that you believe need further development to help you conquer stress. Reviewing the results of the self-assessment questionnaires may help this process. Review also the notes you may have made at the end of each chapter.

After completing Activity 21 you will have a list of areas that you may wish to work on to help you conquer stress. The next stage is to write up your Action Plan. A helpful strategy is to break down the process into the three key areas: psychological, behavioural and health. To help you we include here a sample plan (see pages 81–3). The Action Plan can be revised and updated as and when necessary.

Once you have developed your Action Plan – ie once you have finished Activity 21 – you will be on the path to becoming a 'stress manager'. However, you will not have quite finished, because you could also become a 'life manager' who plans ahead and does not leave important issues to chance. For more on this, see Activity 22 on pages 83–4.

SAMPLE ACTION PLAN

Action to be taken by: Jayne   **Date**: 28 February

1 Psychological

Thinking skills   Stop making mountains out of molehills! Keep events in perspective: life's a hassle but seldom a horror!

Quit holding on to rigid, demanding 'musts' and 'shoulds'. This will reduce the pressure upon me, my family and staff.

Remember that I am not my behaviour! If I fail at some task, it does not mean that I'm a total failure.

Imagery skills   If life gets on top of me, use time projection imagery to remind myself that in a few months' time the situation won't seem so bad.

2 Behavioural

Social support   Make an effort to cultivate more colleagues at work. Have a few more non-work-related chats to people This needn't take up much extra time. I'll start taking tea breaks and chat then.

Start regularly going out to the cinema again with my partner. Ensure we go out with friends at least once a month.

Assertiveness   Practise saying no. Start thinking of the consequences of taking on additional work before answering positively to my colleagues' requests.

Make a big effort to reduce my whinging to my colleagues and partner, and stop blaming others so often.

Time management   Avoid procrastinating! Remind myself that my boss only wants a good job done and not 110 per cent. I elevate tasks into burdens with my thinking errors.

3 Physical health

Exercise   Incorporate exercise into my daily routine: three days a week I'll walk to work; at least once a day I'll use the stairs at work and not the lift; I'll take up badminton again and play at weekends.

Nutrition	I'll eat red meat once a week only. I'll attempt to eat fish three times a week.
	If I fancy a snack, I'll eat some fruit.
	I'll give semi-skimmed milk a try for two weeks. If I get used to the taste then I'll continue. I'll drink less coffee and more tea instead.
Relaxation	Before bedtime I'll spend 10 minutes using relaxation imagery. At work I'll 'make' the opportunity to use relaxation imagery just before I go home to help me switch off and leave my work stresses where they belong – at work.

Activity 22 The future

Have you thought about your future? Think about how you might deal with any of the following life events that may conceivably apply to you:

- partner leaves you
- partner becomes seriously ill or dies
- close friend or family member dies
- birth of a child or children
- child or children start school
- child or children finish school
- adult child leaves home
- you receive promotion or demotion

- losing or changing jobs
- long-term unemployment
- physical disability or illness
- encounter sexual difficulties
- change in residence

The life manager may spend a few minutes every month thinking about how to deal with a range of difficult issues. They may update their CVs every three months and decide whether they need more training or need to move into a new area of work. If problems crop up at work, they are already prepared for action. On retirement, they are unlikely to retire to the country or a dormitory seaside town without first ensuring that they know the place well, perhaps even spending many weekends there over a period of years in order to develop a support network of friends before deciding to make the final move. Although children are very important to them, life manager couples will have ensured that they have maintained a good relationship with each other and put aside time for themselves, so that when the children finally leave home they do not experience an overwhelming sense of loss and do not need to overhaul their relationship.

Start now

Reading a book on stress management is the easy part. Armchair stress experts exist all over the world. Use the motivation imagery exercise on page 50 and think of the benefits to you, your family and colleagues. The best way to conquer stress is to start now and not leave it to chance. *You can do it*!

appendix

1   Useful organisations

American Academy of Experts in Traumatic Stress
368 Veterans Memorial Highway
Commack
New York 11725, USA
Telephone: +1 516 543 2217
Website: www.aaets.org

Holds an international register of experts in stress management, traumatic stress and bereavement. Publishes useful material on trauma.

British Association for Counselling
1 Regent Place
Warwickshire, CV21 2PJ, England
Administration telephone: +44 (0) 1788 550899
Information telephone: +44 (0) 1788 578328

Provides list of accredited counsellors and relevant organisations.

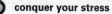

British Association for Behavioural and Cognitive Psychotherapies
PO Box 9
Accrington, BB5 2GD, England
Telephone: +44 (0) 1254 875277
Website: www.babcp.org.uk

Provides a list of accredited cognitive–behavioural and rational–emotive therapists. These approaches focus on a person's unhelpful thinking and behaviours, which is similar to the approach advocated by this book.

British Psychological Society
St Andrews House
48 Princes Road East
Leicester, LE1 7DR, England
Telephone: +44 (0) 116 254 9568
website: www.bps.org.uk

Holds a register of chartered psychologists and publishes a range of books.

Centre for Stress Management
156 Westcombe Hill
London, SE3 7DH, England
Telephone: +44 (0) 20 8853 1122
Website: www.managingstress.com

Provides stress counselling, coaching and training services, and undertakes stress audits and interventions at work. Has mail-order service of relevant stress management and health-related books. It runs distance learning programmes and stress management courses using the approach advocated by this book.

International Stress Management Association
PO Box 348
Waltham Cross, EN8 8XL, England
Telephone: +44 (0) 7000 780430
Website: www.isma.org.uk

Provides information about stress management and accredits members.

Chartered Institute of Personnel and Development
CIPD House
Camp Road
London, SW19 4UX, England
Telephone: +44 (0) 20 8971 9000
Website: www.cipd.co.uk

Professional body that publishes a range of useful books and materials.

Robertson Cooper Ltd
The Fairbarn Building
UMIST
PO Box 88
Manchester, M60 1QD, England
Telephone: +44 (0) 161 200 4562

Stress audits/consultancy and applied research.

2   Bibliography

BENSON H. *The Relaxation Response*. London, Collins, 1976.

CLARKE D. *and* PALMER S. *Stress Management Trainer's Guide*. Cambridge, National Extension College, 1994.

COOPER C. L., COOPER R. D. *and* EAKER L. H. *Living with Stress*. Harmondsworth, Penguin, 1988.

ELLIS A., GORDON J., NEENAN M. *and* PALMER S. *Stress Counseling: A rational emotive behaviour approach*. New York, Springer Publishing Company, 1998.

GEE PUBLISHING. *A–Z of Absence: An audit of cost-reduction procedures*. London, Gee Publishing, 1999.

PALMER S. 'Assertion'. *Journal for Women in the GMB, Northern Region*, 1990.

PALMER S. 'Self-acceptance: concept, techniques and interventions'. *The Rational Emotive Behaviour Therapist*. 5, 1. pp4–30. 1997.

PALMER S. 'The negative travel beliefs questionnaire (NTBQ)'. *The Rational Emotive Behaviour Therapist*. 7, 1. pp48–51. 1999.

PALMER S. *and* DRYDEN W. *Counselling for Stress Problems*. London, Sage, 1995.

PALMER S. *and* NEENAN M. 'Double imagery procedure'. *The Rational Emotive Behaviour Therapist*. 6, 2. pp89–92. 1998.

PALMER S. *and* STRICKLAND L. *Stress Management: A quick guide*. Dunstable, Folens, 1996.

3   Further reading

BOR R., JOSSE J. *and* PALMER S. *Stress-Free Flying*. Dinton, Mark Allen Publishing, 2000.

CLARKE D. *and* PALMER S. *How to Manage Stress*. Cambridge, National Extension College, 1994.

EARNSHAW J. *and* COOPER C. *Stress and Employer Liability*. London, Institute of Personnel and Development, 1996.

ELLIS A. *and* HARPER R. A. *A Guide to Rational Living*. Hollywood, CA, Wilshire, 1997.

GILLEN T. *Assertiveness*. London, Institute of Personnel and Development, 1998.

HAUCK P. *Calm Down: How to cope with frustration and anger*. London, Sheldon Press, 1980.

MAITLAND I. *Managing Your Time*. London, Institute of Personnel and Development, 1995.

PALMER S. *and* BURTON T. *Dealing with People Problems at Work*. Maidenhead, McGraw-Hill, 1996.

PALMER S. *and* STRICKLAND L. *Stress Management: A quick guide*. Dunstable, Folens, 1996.